ECCLESIASTICAL "WOLVES" IN SHEEP'S CLOTHING

The acceptance and propagation of
Protestant Ecclesiology among
Baptist preachers have put
God's people on a road
that leads back
to Rome!

THE DOCTRINE OF THE CHURCH

THE ORIGIN & NATURE

OF

BAPTIST CHURCHES

[Baptists] They are like the river Rhone, which sometimes flows as a river broad and deep, but at other times is hidden in the sands. It, however, never loses its continuity or existence. It is simply hidden for a period. Baptist churches may disappear and re-appear in the most unaccountable manner. Persecuted everywhere by sword and by fire, their principles would appear to be almost extinct, when in a most wondrous way God would raise up some man, or some company of martyrs, to proclaim the truth. The footsteps of the Baptists of the ages can more easily be traced by blood than by baptism. It is a lineage of suffering more than a succession of bishops; a martyrdom of principle, rather than a dogmatic decree of councils; a golden chord of love, rather than an iron chain of succession, which, while attempting to rattle its links back to the apostles, has been of more service in chaining some protesting Baptist to the stake than in proclaiming the truth of the New Testament. It is, nevertheless, a right royal succession, that in every age the Baptists have been advocates of liberty for all, and have held that the gospel of the Son of God makes every man a free man in Christ Jesus.

John T. Christian

3

CHAPTERS

THE DOCTRINE OF THE CHURCH

It is heartbreaking today to witness the destruction and disregard of Baptist history and heritage. It is a sad assessment, but an honest one that the average Baptist church member is woefully uneducated concerning Baptist Doctrines, Distinctives, and Discipline. Who's at fault? There isn't one single factor, person, or group to blame. Certainly, the enemy wants to sever Baptists from their ancient history and the Bible doctrines that make us distinctively different as Bible believing Baptists. Satan would love to divorce us from the truths that certify Bible believing Baptists as the True Churches of Christ, His Bride. However, far too many of those claiming the name "Baptist" have most certainly stayed the enemy's hand and have in ignorance assisted in the scheme of the anti-Christ to make invisible on this earth the True Visible Churches of Christ by assimilation and association with unbiblical churches, and acceptance and propagation of unbiblical doctrines. Most Baptists do not appreciate or know why they are Baptist, and the enemy loves it. Far too many "Baptist" preachers have disregarded Bible doctrine, which is Baptist doctrine, and have embraced the notion that fellowship trumps truth. Many are far too willing and ready to ignore doctrine for ecclesiastical fellowship with groups that are not scriptural. This is not a moral assessment of any person, but a doctrinal one. Faith and facts have been sacrificed at the altar of feelings. Worship has been demoted and emotionalism deified. Even among our own there are those who are ready to claim a church dead if it doesn't meet "their" standard of what worship should be.

There was a time when Baptists understood their ancient ancestry; they understood their history began during the ministry of Christ and that His Church has never ceased to exist. Charles Spurgeon said,

"All who know much of the Baptist denomination must have regretted that so few are acquainted with its early history...it remains a matter of great surprise that our own congregations should be, for the most part, uninstructed in the past doings of our body."[1]

James R. Beller makes the following statement concerning the severance of Baptist from their Ancient Ancestry in *The Coming Destruction of the Baptist People*,

"Until 1899, every Baptist historian in the world acknowledged the Baptists as ancient people tracing their principles back to Christ and His

---

[1] Spurgeon, Charles., *The Sword and the Trowel*, August 1868.

disciples. Every Baptist historian held this view. If Spurgeon was surprised in his day that congregations were uninstructed, he would be shocked to know in our day, neither congregation nor pastors are instructed."[1] Beller provides a list of Baptist historians who believed Baptists to be ancient:

➢ John Spittlehouse (1652)

➢ Theilman J. Van Braught (1660)

➢ Henry D'Anvers (1670)

➢ Thomas Crosby (1740)

➢ Isaac Backus (1770)

➢ David Benedict (1813)

➢ Joseph Ivimey (1830)

➢ G. H. Orchard (1830)

➢ J. M. Cramp (1868)

➢ William Cathcart (1887)

➢ Thomas Armitage (1888)

➢ J. M. Carroll (1901)

➢ John Taylor Christian (1926)

---

[1] Beller, James. R., *The Coming Destruction of the Baptist People*, pg. 1-2, Prairie Fire Press.

It is an unmitigated truth that the Lord's Church began prior to Pentecost. The True Churches of Christ never associated or gave in to the satanic demands of the harlot Church of Rome or her Protestant daughters. Therefore, Baptists are not Protestant. At least not scripturally or through the eyes of ancient and accurate history. Sadly, the average "Baptist" has accepted the modern idea that their faith, the faith once delivered unto the saints, is a product of the Reformation. Apparently what Jesus failed to do in keeping the "gates of hell" from prevailing against His Church, He needed Wesley, Calvin and Luther's help with! They now cheerfully embrace ecclesiastically those groups which once opposed and persecuted our ancestors. Not only have they tied themselves to the Protestant Faith, but they have also begun to embrace Protestant fallacies concerning the origin and nature of the Church. Why wouldn't they? One departure leads to another, then another and so on until the doctrines that make us distinctly God's chosen are so blurred that there is no longer any distinction at all. The only requirement left in the minds of most for being accepted of God is to be sincere. But sincerity never made anyone right, and many are sincerely wrong.

"Prior to the Reformation our Baptist predecessors were very careful about the authority by whom those had been baptized who came to them from other societies. These principles are not consistently practiced by Protestant churches, and even Baptists who accept Protestant origins are becoming careless about some of them. This is the danger. Once compromise begins, it is so easy for it to continue."[1]

[1] Cross, I.K., *The Battle for Baptist History*, Bogard Press, pg. 124.

THE ORIGIN OF THE CHURCH

To find the origin of the Lord's Church, it must be determined which "church" we are referring to. Which question itself implies another, is there more than one church? A drive through most towns would lead the average person to say "Yes," there are several different "churches." And, in the truest sense of the New Testament word *ekklesia* as it was used when "Holy men of God spake as they were moved by the Holy Ghost," there are different "churches." But only in the sense of the word *ekklesia,* which means "assembly," but does not necessarily imply the reason for the assembly. Many groups assemble together and take the title "church," which in the minds of most people implies a connection to Christianity. But an honest interrogation of the beliefs of these assemblies will obviously show there are great differences in doctrine and practice. There is no doubt to the sincerity of each group. However, can each group having different beliefs with different origins each make the claim to be the Church of Christ? Did Christ not establish a Church? Did Christ not teach His Church? If He did, as He most certainly did, would it not then matter what a "church" believes and practices? Would it not matter the origin of each grouping laying claim to the honor of being the or a

Church of Christ? I submit that it does, as Christ would not organize groups opposing each other in doctrine in practice. Nor would He having organized His own Church be satisfied with any other being organized at a later date and established on principles foreign to those found in the New Testament. So that, while there are different "churches" in the sense of the word *ekklesia* meaning "assembly," there can only be one True Church *(The aggregate of all true churches)* belonging to the Lord. Many people are offended by the assertions I have made. The only qualification in the minds of the average Christian is that a person be sincere, and to that extent, for a "church" to be sincere in order to be accepted as biblical. J.R. Graves stated,

"The fact that a man or society has accomplished a large amount of good is not sufficient to prove that he is Christian, or that such a society is a Church of Christ, or entitled to the name of Church."[1]

However, these statements are as biblical as they are logical.

---

[1] Graves, J.R. *The Great Iron Wheel, or Republicanism Backwards and Christianity Reversed*, pg. 13, Forgotten Books.

"Things equal to or like the same thing are equal to or like each other. Corollary – If these fifty different and conflicting organizations, claiming to be churches, are each *evangelical, i.e., scriptural,* they must be like each other in doctrine and organization; but they are essentially and radically unlike the one to the other, and therefore they cannot all be *scriptural.*"[1]

It then becomes the prerogative of every born-again believer to "rightly divide the word of truth" in order to identify and associate himself scripturally with a New Testament church as found in the Word of God. J.R. Graves, in a series of letters addressed to J. Soule, Bishop of Methodist Episcopal Church states it this way,

"But Alas, sir, how fearful to you now would be the thought, that you have exhausted the whole of life, hazarded all those dangers, underwent all those toils to advance the interests of an organization, not instituted by Christ, or authorized by His word – but a mere human, man-devised system – a rival fold, whose very being and advancement is hostile to, and subversive of, the Church and Kingdom of Christ, set up by Him and designed to fill the

---

1 Graves. J.R. *Old Landmarkism: What is It?* , pg. 12, Solid Christian Books.

13

whole world! What an awful thought for an aged minister about to die, that he has spent his long life and exhausted all his mighty powers of mind and body in opposing the Kingdom of Christ, and diverting those seeking to enter in into a rival organization, which, becoming universal, would blot out the doctrines, constitution, and very being of Christ's Church from the world!!"[1]

Jesus said, "I will build my church; and the gates of hell shall not prevail against it" (Matt. 16:18). There are two absolute truths revealed in this statement. 1) That Jesus was the founder of His Church; 2) That the Church established by Christ was "His" Church, and that the Church established by Christ would have a continual existence from its conception to His return.

First, Jesus emphatically stated, "I will build my church." Now notice the world "build." Of Course, that faction of Christians who believe the Church began on Pentecost as opposed to the Lord's Church finding its origin in His personal ministry refer to this verse as proof positive by asserting that the word "build" has only a future reference; that this passage indicates that the Church was not present

---

[1] Graves. J. R. *The Great Iron Wheel, or Republicansim Backwards and Christianity Reversed*, pg. 13, Forgotten Books.

14

during His ministry but would be birthed on Pentecost. By asserting this, they put themselves in a position to explain how Christ could build a church at a time when He wasn't present. The word "build" here does have a future application but does not suggest the non-existence of the Church at this point, but rather that Christ would continue to build, to build up, to edify, or to strengthen. That this work began by Christ carries on through the ministry of the Holy Spirit is conceded. However, Jesus established His Church during His personal ministry on earth. Consider the following:

➢ The Apostles were the first gifts to the Church and were installed, becoming the foundation of the Church, during the ministry of Christ. (1st Corinthians 12:28; Mark 3:13-14; Ephesians 2:19-20)

➢ The church was added to on the day of Pentecost. (Acts 2:41)

➢ The Lord sang with His church. (Hebrews 2:12; Matt. 26:30) Notice the reference in Hebrews is a restatement of a Messianic prophecy in Psalm 22:22, "I will declare thy name unto my brethren: in the midst of the congregation will I praise thee." It's important to note that the Bible interprets for us a church as an "assembly" or "congregation" by comparing Psalm 22:22 & Hebrews 2:12. The only recorded instance we have of Jesus singing in the New Testament was prior to Pentecost, when after instituting His memorial supper they, "sung an hymn" Matt. 26:30.

➤ The Lord gave the "Great Commission" prior to Pentecost. (Matt 28:18-20)

➤ The Lord instituted and observed His memorial supper prior to Pentecost. (Matt. 26:20-30)

➤ The Lord gave disciplinary authority prior to Pentecost. (Matt: 18:15-20) Notice that this is the second mention of the Church in the New Testament, and that it is clearly mentioned in reference to, and has no application outside of that of a local assembly of believers.

Then there are those that say, "The True Church is *Universal* and is found within all the local 'churches' without regard to denomination." This assertion is as foreign to scripture as it is obnoxious. As I will expand on this Protestant fallacy later, let me refer you again to the Greek word selected by the Holy Spirit of God, *ekklesia*, which means "assembly."

The *Church Universal* is an oxymoron, as it is a concept made up of contradictory and incongruous words and elements. An *assembly* cannot be present everywhere, nor can something *universal* ever be assembled together anywhere. The word "church" here is used by synecdoche, or the general/institutional sense. That is, all churches in general but no church in particular, or simply in the sense of an institution as it is used in a few other places, i.e., Ephesians 5:25. Jesus then is the Founder of "His" church, and a "church" whose founder is any other than Jesus cannot be the Church built by Christ.

Secondly, the Church established by Jesus is "His" Church. That is to say, it belongs to Him, He is the Founder, Head, and only Lawgiver to His Church. Jesus has a Church; He must, for He said, "I will build my church, and the gates of hell shall not prevail against it." It follows then that not only did Christ establish His Church, but that the Church belongs to Him and would continue to exist from conception until the Lord's return. There are many assemblies of people today who claim to be a "church" of Christ but fail to produce historical ties to first century Christianity. If Jesus started His Church, it then necessarily follows any "church" who finds its origin with man fails to

17

meet the criteria for being the Church of Christ. A quick survey of the history of the Reformation will provide the origin for most of the "churches" in existence today *(Notice chart in back of booklet).* It is however asserted by some that Baptists as well are Protestant and therefore have no history anymore ancient than that of their own *(This is sadly the common view of many Bapto-Protestants today).*

Sadly, many well-meaning Baptists today know nothing of their own ancient history and have accepted the notion that we (Baptists) are Protestant. What was not started by Jesus but was set up by man in opposition to "His" Church cannot therefore be "His" Church. "History is messy," as James A. Patterson stated when disputing the claims of Baptist Secessionism while chronicling the life of Baptist secessionist J.R. Graves.[1] Patterson went on to defend the William Whitsitt *English Descent Theory*[2] of Baptist origin by saying,

---

[1] Patterson, James A., *James Robinson Graves: Staking the Boundaries of Baptist Identity,* pg. 119, Studies in Baptist Life and Thought.

[2] *Baptist began around 1641 from English separatists, and are therefore Protestant (falsely so called}

18

"Graves spawned further efforts to perpetuate a bogus denominational identity, which only intensified a mistaken understanding of the relationship of faith and history among Baptists. A few years after Grave's death, a muddled conception of Baptist history and identity contributed to the severe reaction that greeted William Whitsitt when he endeavored to apply earnest historical scholarship to the issue of Baptist origins. Secessionist apologetics reached a nadir with *The Trial of Blood*, but there were others like New Orleans professor John T. Christian (1854-1925) who offered a somewhat more sophisticated version. Untimely, Grave's subordination of history to ecclesiology dealt a troublesome setback to the Baptist historical enterprise. After carefully assessing the secessionist legacy, Baptists who are serious about history might well wonder whether they have been victims of identity theft."[1]

Modern Baptist Historian James Beller on the other hand writes concerning the inconsistency of Whitsett's theory,

"In the spring of 1896, William Whitsitt wrote an article about the Baptists for *Johnson's*

---

[1] Patterson, James A., *James Robinson Graves: Staking the Boundaries of Baptist Identity*, pg. 119, Studies in Baptist Life and Thought.

Encyclopedia. The article stated his theory that the English Baptists did not begin to baptize by immersion until 1641, when a portion of the "Ana-Baptist" began immersing. (Note)[1] The 'Theory of 1641' set off a firestorm of opposition. Henry M. King of Rhode Island; Dr. J. H. Spencer, the Kentucky Baptist historian; and Dr. T. T. Eaton, editor of the *Western Recorder* immediately responded to Whitsitt. It was revealed that Dr. Whitsitt, was the author of the infamous but now almost forgotten set of articles, which appear in the *New York Independent* in 1880. John Taylor Christian, a Baptist pastor in Mississippi, began to study the files of the *Independent* and found other editorials in which the Baptist were attacked. It

---

[1] W.A. Jarrel quotes Presbyterian Professor Dr. Philip Schaff saying, "The history of the Anabaptists of the Reformation period has yet to be written from an impartial, unsectarian standpoint. The polemical attitude of the reformers against them has warped the judgment of historians. They were cruelly treated in their lifetime by the Romanists and Protestants, and misrepresented after their death as a set of heretical and revolutionary fanatics who could not be tolerated in a Christian state. The excesses of a misguided faction have been charged upon the whole body." Jarrel states, *"There was a great difference between the Anabaptists and the Anabaptists. There were those among them who held strange doctrines, but this cannot be said of the whole sect."* Anabaptist was a name given to almost any group who dissented and stood against Rome and her daughters. (Pgs. 226 & 232-233, *Baptist Church Perpetuity.* W. A. Jarrel.) Just as there are differences among "Baptists" today, some obviously heretical, there were those differences then among those called "Anabaptists." They were not all, nor were the majority of them, heretical!

was clear that Whitsitt undermined the principles of the Baptists while being employed by the sacrifices of Baptist people. Whitsitt wrote, '...if in the future it shall ever be made to appear that I have erred in my conclusions, I would promptly and cheerfully say so.' ...... In Ford's *Christian Repository*, for January of 1897, Dr. Joseph Angus, famed English Baptist preacher and writer cited the existence of 26 Baptist churches practicing immersion before 1641. Perhaps most telling, he gave the names of at least 21 pamphlets opposing the 'dippers' (Baptists) and their manner of IMMERSION, all written before 1641. Mr. Whitsitt never did admit his error and was dismissed from Southern Baptist Seminary In 1898. However his 'anti-christian' forgery became accepted after his death. His 'English Descent Theory' became the official stance of the Southern Baptist Convention. In 1905, A large number of Baptists disagreed with the Whitsitt stance, withdrew from the convention, and formed the American Baptist Association. (Landmark Baptist) ......Whitsittism insisted the Baptist did *not exist* until the Reformation. It was the tool of the *adversary* used to reconstruct the Southern Baptists of America into Protestants. (Note)[1] Since the Independent Baptist share a mutual history with the Southern Baptist, it has affected them also. It was the blow that severed ties with the ancient Baptist."[2]

Dr. William H. Whitsitt "made an error in his conclusions as a result of his historical research that has polluted the stream of Baptist

---

[1]Les Potter explains this connection in *Baptist Baptism: A Heritage of Scriptural Authority Vs. The Corruption of Popular Practice*, (pg. 8-9). "In generations not too distant, the striding gains of apostasy and modernism caused a backlash of reaction among conservative Protestants. A fledgling movement drew a minority within various denominations who banded together under the flag of Fundamentalism. Their tune of militancy for the faith was welcome among those who had seen the decline of its fervency in America. It rang loudly in the Baptist camp also; resting from centuries of persecution by Catholicism and Protestant reformers alike. Nevertheless, many clung to the optimistic thought that the true root of Fundamentalism was fidelity to every word of the King James Bible. They thought this root would ultimately prevail to the purifying of their mingled movement. While (Fundamental Baptist) declared fidelity to Baptist identity, the fruit of their spiritual fornication produced a generation that spake with a Baptist tongue and a Protestant dictionary. Thus, the lessons of scripture and history are repeatedly demonstrated. Fundamentalism did not produce Baptists from Protestants. It produced Protestants with a Baptist name. What centuries of persecution could not do, The Trojan horse of Fundamentalism did magnificently. We now find ourselves once again defending the same Biblical truths for which Baptist Martyrs suffered. Today, however, it is with brethren that identify with our name and heritage who despise the Bible doctrine that distinguished both."

[2] Beller, James R., *The Coming Destruction of Baptist People*, pg. 22-24, Prairie Fire Press

history until this day ... he introduced a fallacy into Baptist history which his successors have picked up and blown into complete revolution that is eating like a termite at the very foundations of our Baptist heritage. As they rewrite Baptist history, Protestant doctrinal concepts are also beginning to be accepted, and their leaders give Dr. Whitsitt credit for what they are doing."[1]

W. A Jarrel writes in *Baptist Church Perpetuity*;

"The only senses in which one Baptist church can succeed another are that the church leads men and women to Christ, then through its missionaries or ministers baptizes them, after which the baptized organize themselves into a Baptist church; or, in lettering off some of its members to organize a new church; or, in the case the old church has fallen to pieces, for its members to reorganize themselves into a church. All that Baptists mean by Church Perpetuity, is: There has never been a day since its organization of the first New Testament

---

[1] Cross, I.K., *The Battle for Baptist History*, Bogard Press, pgs. 131&137.

23

church in which there was no genuine church of the New Testament existing on earth."[1]

But as it stands today Patterson and many others, without a doubt the overwhelming majority reject the secessionist view of Baptist History and identity but seem to do so for what they perceive is a lack of historical evidence. History it seems, as Patterson stated, is "messy." And, history is often if not most often reported from a slanted perspective. And so, it seems to become the responsibility of the secessionist prove the succession theory, but only so far as those who disagree have failed to disprove it. However, I do not feel the need to prove this view historically, so long as it has not been disproved, which in my mind and estimation may be impossible to do to the satisfaction of those whose minds are made up, in so far as history is muddled, messy and most often biased. As James Beller stated,

"No historian is able to give facts alone. I say the historian cannot hide his heart."[2]

---

[1] Jarrel, W.A., *Baptist Church Perpetuity*, The Baptist History Series, pg. 2-3, The Baptist Standard Bearer.

[2] Beller, James R., *America in Crimson Red: The Baptist History in America*, pg. xv, Prairie Fire Press.

However, Landmarkers do believe it to be an unmitigated truth that the Lord established His church and that Church has continued in unbroken succession from the time of Christ until today, and had history been thoroughly and accurately recorded it would prove the same. W. A. Jarrel in *Baptist Church Perpetuity* quotes Dr. Benedict, a Baptist Historian,

"The more I study the subject the stronger are my convictions that if all the facts in the case could be disclosed a very good case could be made out."[1]

John T. Christian states concerning Baptist history;

"I have no question in my own mind that there has been a historical succession of Baptist churches from the days of Christ to the present time."[2]

However, secessionist believe this because it was the promise of Christ, "the gates of Hell shall not prevail against it." This is the promise of the perpetuity of the Church and had the whole of the historical account said otherwise

---

[1] Jarrel, W. A., *Baptist Church Perpetuity*, The Baptist History Series, pg. 39, The Baptist Standard Bearer.

[2] Christian, John T., *A History of the Baptists*, Volume One., pg. 5-6. Bogard Press.

we'd still believe the promise of Christ; knowing history was written by man, but this was the promise of Christ. "The more earnestly the [Baptists] adhered to Scriptural principles the less likely was mention made of them. It was the unusual and the heretical that attracted attention and was recorded in the histories of the times."[1]

I give one biblical example where history fails to prove a known biblical fact. The bible teaches that man is a sinner because his father Adam was a sinner. Yet no man can trace themselves in a genealogical way by chain link back to Adam and yet we believe it because the evidence is clear before us that we are the descendants of Adam bearing the marks of sin, and more emphatically so because the Bible declares us sinners originating with and in Adam. If others, as I do, accept this biblical truth without being able to confirm it historically, why are secessionist compelled to prove the promise of Christ Historically. Is there not a church in the world today that is built on the principles of Christ found in the New Testament, bearing the marks of the New Testament Church? Yes! Then what other proof

---

[1] Christian, John T., *A History of the Baptists*, Volume One., pg. 26, Bogard Press.

26

is needed that Christ honored his promise that the "gates of hell shall not prevail" against His Church? As J.M. Pendleton stated,

"Baptists are not dependent on the testimony of church historians. They make their appeal to the New Testament of our Lord and Saviour Jesus Christ."[1]

I.K. Cross states,

"It is not necessary to show from history that the church of Jesus Christ has continued from the time it was founded until the present. His promise alone makes that certain. However, it puts iron in the blood of real Baptists to be able to demonstrate it from history; to witness the progress of that promise as it is kept under all conditions as history progresses."[2]

Joseph Hooke, 17th century Baptist Preacher wrote,

"But we think it sufficient, that we can prove all we teach by the infallible Records of God's Word, and if all histories and monuments of antiquity had been overlaid, or burnt, as many have been,

---

1 Pendleton, James. M., *Distinctive Principles of Baptists*, pg. 210, Philadelphia: American Baptist Publication Society, The Baptist Standard Bearer, Inc.

2 Cross, I.K., *The Battle for Baptist History*, Bogard Press, pg. 177.

so that we had never been able to shew from any book but the Bible, that there were ever any of our persuasion in the world, till within a few years, yet we should think that book enough to prove the antiquity of our persuasion, that we are not a new sect, seeing that we can make it appear by that one book, that our persuasion is as old as Christ and the Apostles. And on the contrary, if we could show from approved history, that multitudes of all ages and nations since the Apostle's days have been of our persuasion, yet if we could not prove by the Word of God, that our persuasion is true, it would signify very little."[1]

In the end, so far as can be determined, some of those who accept the *English Descent Theory* and all I would hope who hold the *Landmark* view of succession accept the Biblical truth that Christ did set His Church up during His personal ministry. The difference then lies in whether the promise of perpetuity was made to a church *local* and *visible* in its nature, or *universal?* In other words, when Jesus said, "I will build my church, and the gates of hell shall not prevail against it," If, as it was, that church was a *local visible body of scripturally baptized*

---

[1] Christian, John T., *A History of the Baptists,* Volume One., Bogard Press, pg. 259.

believers, then churches of that same nature and order, with the same authority, power and baptism; churches with same government and discipline have never ceased to exist. And this is true whether or not it can be proven historically.

"In the dark ages of Popery, God never 'left Himself without a witness.' It is true that from the rise of that anti-Christian power till the dawn of the reformation, the people of Christ may be emphatically denominated a 'little flock,' yet small as their number may appear to have been to the eye of man, and unable as historians may be, to trace with accuracy the saints of the Most High, amidst 'a world lying in wickedness,' it cannot be doubted that even then, there was a remnant, which kept the commandments of God, and the testimony of Jesus Christ. *If God reserved to Himself 'seven thousand in Israel who had not bowed the knee to Baal,' in the reign of idolatrous Ahab, can we suppose, that during any preceding period, His Church has ceased to exist, or that His cause has utterly perished?*"[1]

[1] Quoted by W. A. Jarrel, *Baptist Church Perpetuity*, pg. 23-24; *History Waldenses,Published by American Sunday School Union*.

WHEN DID THE NEW TESTAMENT BEGIN?

The New Testament Church as established by Christ is not a continuation of something old, but a new establishment, a new organization, a living organism. To speak to one more "theory" concerning the origin of the Lord's Church, it has been proposed that the Church's conception could not be found during the ministry of Christ because the New Testament didn't begin until Pentecost. But the New Testament did not begin on Pentecost as we will see. Based on a false interpretation of Hebrews 9:16-17, some have placed the beginning of the New Testament at Jesus' death on Calvary. Others assume the New Testament began on Pentecost. As a result of this, many believe that the Church began on Pentecost. "For where a testament *is*, there must also of necessity by the death of the testator. For a testament is of force after men are dead: otherwise it is of no strength while the testator liveth" (Hebrews 9:16-17). The word "testament" used here can be thought of as a will. We are all familiar with wills and we know that a will, although in existence, is not in effect until the death of the one who made it. Notice carefully that the writer of Hebrews said, "where a testament is." He did not say, "where a testament was," or even, "where a testament will be," but "where a testament is." The testament was already in place and necessitated the death of the testator (Jesus Christ.) Notice that nowhere in these verses does it say that there is no New Testament until the death of Christ, but rather that the coming of the New Testament demanded the death of Jesus, and that the New Testament, although already present was not in force, or had not come in power until after the death of Jesus. "For a testament is of force after men are dead" (Hebrews 9:17).

The New Testament Church received power on the Day of Pentecost but did not begin on that day. Jesus commanded His church in Luke 24:49, "And, behold, I send the promise of my Father upon you: but tarry ye in the city of Jerusalem, until ye be endued with power from on high." In Acts 1:8 we have recorded, "But ye shall receive power, after that the Holy Ghost is come upon you: and ye shall be witnesses unto me both in Jerusalem, and in all Judaea, and in Samaria, and unto the uttermost part of the earth." This is exactly what happened on the Day of Pentecost; the church received power to fulfill the Commission previously given By Christ. There is no mention of the Church beginning on Pentecost. The Church was however added to on the Day of Pentecost. "And the Lord added to the church" (Acts 2:41).

The New Testament Church began during the earthly ministry of Christ; it began almost as soon as the New Testament itself which was ushered in through the ministry of John the Baptist. "For all the prophets and the law prophesied until John" (Matthew 11:13). The Law and the Prophets spoken of here are in reference to the Old Testament which Jesus said were "until John." Mark 1:1-2 states, "THE beginning of the gospel of Jesus Christ, the Son of God; As it is written in the prophets, Behold, I send my messenger before thy face, which shall prepare thy way before thee. The voice of one crying in the wilderness, Prepare ye the way of the Lord, make his paths straight." John the Baptist's ministry was the beginning of the gospel of Jesus Christ, for he was sent to prepare the way for the coming of the Saviour.

"With the appearance of John the Baptist we have the burial of the Old Dispensation and the emergence of the New. We seem to see his rugged figure standing with arms outstretched, as with one hand he takes the Old Testament, and with the other holds the New, and who, through his ministry, makes the transition from the Law to Grace. He was the foreclosure of the old and the forerunner of the new"[1] Herbert Lockyer.

Is it enough for a church, as Landmark Baptist do, to claim the "glorious inheritance of perpetuity" to also by virtue of this claim be entitled to the name of Christ "unless identical in structure?" It certainly is not! That church must then prove its organizational, structural and doctrinal integrity. Baptists, more specifically Landmark Baptists, bear the biblical marks of a true New Testament Church. This is not to be misunderstood to insist all Baptist churches are scriptural, as many today are moving far away from the New Testament model, but it is to insist that churches scriptural in their doctrine are Baptist. While it is true that there are many churches "Baptist" in name but not in doctrine, there are none scriptural in doctrine that are ashamed to be called Baptist.

---

[1] Lockyer, Herbert. D.D., D.Litt., *All the Men of the Bible*, Zondervan Publishing House 1958.

THE NATURE OF A NEW TESTAMENT CHURCH

To begin discussing the nature of a New Testament Church, it needs to be expressed the importance of a Biblical understanding of what a church is. What a person or group believes concerning the nature of the Church dictates to a large extent the practices of that church. For instance, if a person accepts the view that the Church is *universal*, he most probably then believes communion should be "open," and at best "close." However, if a person believes the Church is *local* and *visible* in nature, he also in accordance practices "closed" communion. Many "Baptists" have accepted the Lutheran notion that all who are redeemed belong to the Lord's church without regard to scriptural baptism. However, some of these same men still have conservative, traditional, biblical practices in place in their churches. Such as, closed communion, only receiving and accepting as valid baptisms those performed in other scriptural Baptist churches and refusing ecclesiastical fellowship with other groups. What led to these practices? The notion that the Church is *Universal?* Surely not. What led to these practices was the scriptural belief that the Church is *local* in nature and Baptist in doctrine. But on what grounds do they restrict any of this if all who are saved are already in the Lord's Church. On one hand they put all the redeemed in the Church, on the other hand they refuse those same people who they have included. The coming generation will no doubt enlarge on this departure. This road that some of our misguided brothers are on will ultimately lead back to Rome!

What is a church? James Pendleton defines a church as,

"A congregation of Christ's baptized disciples, acknowledging him as their Head, relying on his atoning sacrifice for justification before God, depending on the Holy Spirit for sanctification, united in the belief of the gospel, agreeing to maintain its ordinances and obey its precepts, meeting together for worship, and cooperating for the extension of Christ's Kingdom in the world. If any prefer an abridgment of this definition, it may be given thus: A church is a congregation of Christ's baptized disciples, united in the belief of what He has, and covenanting to do what He has commanded."[1]

The question is not whether Pendleton, Graves, or another other preacher past or

---

[1] Pendleton, James M., *Christian Doctrine, A Compendium of Christian Theology*, pg. 282, Judson Press.

modern understands the Church in a *universal* sense, but rather does the Bible teach so! What does, "thus saith the Lord?" Notice the following expressions of belief concerning the nature of the Lord's Church:

1632 Dordrecht Mennonite Confession of Faith – We believe in, and confess a visible church of God, namely, those who, as has been said before, truly repent and believe, and are rightly baptized; who are one with God in heaven, and are rightly incorporated into the communion of saints here on earth."

1644 First London Confession (Baptist) – "That Christ has here on earth a spiritual Kingdom, which is the Church, which He has purchased and redeemed to Himself, as a particular inheritance: which Church, as it is visible to us, is a company of visible saints, called and separated from the world, by Word and the Spirit of God, to a visible profession of faith of the Gospel, being baptized into the faith, and joined to the Lord, and each other, by mutual agreement, in the practical enjoyment of the ordinances, commanded by Christ their head and King.

1800 Doctrinal Statement Green River Association Kentucky – We believe that the visible Church of Christ is a congregation of faithful persons, who have obtained fellowship with each other and have given themselves up to the Lord and one another, having agreed to keep up a godly discipline according to the rules of the Gospel.

John Smyth's 1609 Confession – That the church of Christ is a company of the faithful; baptized after confession of sin and faith, endowed with the power of Christ.

1816 Sandy Creek Association Confession – The visible Church of Christ is a congregation of faithful persons, who have obtained fellowship with each other, and have given themselves up the Lord and one another; having agreed to keep up a godly discipline, according to the rules of the gospel.

New Hampshire Confession 1833 – Of a Gospel Church we believe that a visible Church of Christ is a congregation of baptized believers associated by covenant in the faith and fellowship of the gospel observing the ordinances of Christ; governed by His laws, and exercising the gifts, rights, and privileges invested in them by His word; that its only scriptural officers are Bishops, and Deacons, whose qualifications, claims, and duties are defined in the Epistles to Timothy and Titus.

J. Newton Brown, editor of the New Hampshire Confession of 1833, wrote these words prior to the beginning of the Landmark movement – Christ has had, for 1800 years past, a visible church in earth-made up of the entire body of particular churches, formed under the general constitution of the New Testament...The term "church" is here used, it will be seen, not for the whole body of elect which is ever invisible on earth[1]

Isaac Backus (Leading Baptist preacher during the time of the American Revolution) – Christ has instituted none but particular churches ... The church spoken of by our Lord in Matthew 18:15-18, is such an one as a brother can tell his grievance to, and whoever thought that could be to any other than a particular community.[2]

Baptist Missionary Association of Mississippi – The establishment of a visible church by Christ Himself during His personal ministry on earth;

---

[1]Quoted by Robert Ashcraft, *Landmarkism Revisited*, Ashcraft publications,2003, pp. 116-117

[2] Quoted by Thomas Williamson, *Landmarkism before J.R. Graves*, Isaac Backus, *"A Discourse Concerning the Materials, the Manner of Building and Power of Organizing of the Church of Christ,"* 1773, pp. 17, 145

and His churches are not now, nor have they ever been, universal or invisible.[1]

American Baptist Association – We believe that Jesus Christ established His church during His ministry on earth and that it is always a local, visible assembly of scripturally baptized believers in covenant relationship to carry out the Commission of the Lord Jesus Christ, and each church is an independent, self-governing body, and no other ecclesiastical body may exercise authority over it. We believe that Jesus Christ gave the Great Commission to the New Testament churches only, and that He promised the perpetuity of His churches (Matt. 4:18-22; Matt. 16:18; Matt. 28:19, 20; Mark 1:14-20; John 1:35-51; Eph. 3:21).[2]

These statements are only a sample of those available. But to provide one more, consider the largest Baptist fellowship in America, the Southern Baptist Convention. In the 1925 edition of the SBC Faith and Message the following definition was given of a church:

1925 Southern Baptist Faith and Message – "A church of Christ is a congregation of baptized believers, associated by covenant in the faith

---

[1] www.bmaofmississippi.com

[2] http://www.bible.ca/cr-american-baptist-association.htm

and fellowship of the gospel; observing the ordinances of Christ, governed by His laws, and exercising the gifts, rights, and privileges invested in them by His word, and seeking to extend the gospel to the ends of the earth. Its Scriptural officers are bishops, or elders, and deacons. *Matt. 16:18; Matt. 18:15-18; Rom. 1:7; 1 Cor. 1:2; Acts 2:41-42; 5:13-14; 2 Cor. 9:13; Phil. 1:1; 1 Tim. 4:14; Acts 14:23;Acts 6:3,5-6; Heb. 13:17; 1 Cor. 9:6,14.*" (There is nothing at all mentioned concerning a *Universal* Church, and this definition is as good as any.)

Then in the 1963 edition the statement was updated to include the Church in a *Universal* sense. James Patterson considers this a triumph over Landmarkism,

"For example, the original 1925 version of the Baptist Faith and Message, which followed the 1833 New Hampshire Confession at many points, defined the New Testament church in local terms only, omitting any reference to the *universal* church. This possible concession to Landmark sentiment, however, seemed dispensable by 1963 when the FMB revision committee added this line"[1] (which is included in italics below)

1963 Southern Baptist Faith and Message – "A New Testament church of the Lord Jesus Christ is a local body of baptized believers who are associated by covenant in the faith and fellowship of the gospel, observing the two ordinances of Christ, committed to His teachings, exercising the gifts, rights, and privileges invested in them by His Word, and seeking to extend the gospel to the ends of the earth.

This church is an autonomous body, operating through democratic processes under the Lordship of Jesus Christ. In such a congregation, members are equally responsible. Its Scriptural officers are pastors and deacons.

The New Testament speaks also of the church as the body of Christ which includes all of the redeemed of all the ages. " (Notice the progression from *local* to *universal*. Yet there is no mention of the false teaching concerning being "baptized by the Spirit into this *universal body*, that will come next.)

---

[1] Patterson, James A., *James Robinson Graves: Staking the Boundaries of Baptist Identity*, pg. 195, Studies in Baptist Life and Thought.

Lastly notice that in 1963 there was no mention of *Baptism by the Holy Ghost* for believers. This was added to the 2000 edition of the Southern Baptist Faith and Message.

"The Holy Spirit is the Spirit of God, fully divine. He inspired holy men of old to write the Scriptures. Through illumination He enables men to understand truth. He exalts Christ. He convicts men of sin, of righteousness, and of judgment. He calls men to the Saviour, and effects regeneration. *At the moment of regeneration, He baptizes every believer into the Body of Christ.* He cultivates Christian character, comforts believers, and bestows the spiritual gifts by which they serve God through His church. He seals the believer unto the day of final redemption. His presence in the Christian is the guarantee that God will bring the believer into the fullness of the stature of Christ. He enlightens and empowers the believer and the church in worship, evangelism, and service."

Now consider the damage this has done within the SBC. In a recent article from the SBC International Missions Board the following is stated,

"How Baptist Churches Have Struggled – While we must plant Baptist churches, we also must avoid insularity while we do so. Regrettably, our tradition has often struggled with this particular vice. Sometimes we've had to guard against the insularity of ignorance. Some Southern Baptists have argued that only Baptist churches are "true" churches, that Baptist-like churches have always existed, and that the presence of said churches at all times and in all places is a biblical necessity. At times, variations of this view and its implications have had a toxic effect on our missionary endeavors. Over the past century, however, the insularity of arrogance has proven to be a greater temptation. Southern Baptists are the largest Protestant denomination in America."[1] Landmarkism, the tenets of which has helped to retain Baptist distinctiveness and identity, is considered to be toxic to many in the SBC today! And yet Landmarkism is nothing new, and nothing but a scriptural interpretation and emphasis concerning the Lord's Church.

Sadly, many SBC churches and Missionary Baptists as well are liberal in their ecclesiology. Many "Baptist" churches now are accepting immersions from non-Baptist

---

[1] www.imb.org, *Why We Plant Baptist Churches*, Nathan Finn., November 15, 2018.

44

churches; many tend to be very ecumenical in their ecclesiology, pulpit affiliation and open communion, etc. What led to this, the idea that the church was *local* and *visible* only, or that the Church is *universal* including the redeemed of all ages? They are at least consistent in their ecclesiology. If you believe everyone who is saved is already in the "church," then what right and what grounds have you to restrict anything? It is ecclesiastical hypocrisy on the one hand to accept the *Universal Church Theory*, but on the other hand be restrictive in the observance of the Ordinances, etc. They embrace Protestant ecclesiology but practice Baptist polity.

The Southern Baptist Convention now boasts of being the *Largest Protestant Denomination* in the world. As it has been shown, they have now always believed themselves to be Protestant, this is a result of accepting the flawed historical theory of William Whitsitt. Landmarkism "grew up with Southern Baptist from their origin. Only in the 20th century has it been rejected by those professors who have chosen to join the ranks of Protestantism are rewrite their history to support their new-found theories."[1]

------

1 Cross, I.K., *The Battle for Baptist History*, Bogard Press, pg. 174.

LOCAL & VISIBLE / UNIVERSAL

Jesus, while on this earth during His personal ministry did establish a Church; His Church. That Church would be the model for all other churches. In fact, all other true churches find their origin in this Church. There are only three ways in which the word "church" is used in the New Testament. 1)To refer to some particular, local, visible body of believers; 2) to refer to a group of churches; 3) to refer to no church in particular, but all churches in general, or in an institutional sense. But the word "church" is never used in a *universal* sense. This belief is the product of the Reformation and the thinking of the reformer Martin Luther who built on the ideas of Augustine. How does anyone come to the pages of scripture and find anything other than a church, or churches, both identifying "assemblies" and leave with the thought the Church is *Universal*? They do so because their minds were made up before they approached the scripture; they do so because of pre-supposition; they do so because some preacher or commentary told them the Church was *Universal*, but not because the scripture identifies it so. W.A. Jarrel quotes E.J. Fish, D.D. as saying;

"All investigation concurs with 'unequivocal uses of the term in pronouncing the actual to be a local society and never anything but a local society.' "The real church of Christ is a local body, of a definite, doctrinal constitution such as is indispensable to the unity of the Spirit." Alluding to its application to all professors, of all creeds, scattered everywhere, as an "invisible," "universal church," Dr. Fish well says: "Not a single case can be adduced where the loose and extended use of the collective can be adopted without a forced and unnatural interpretation. The New Testament is utterly innocent of the inward conflict of those theories which adopt both the invisible, or universal, as it is now more commonly called, and the local ideas."[1]

Where then did the idea of the Church *Universal* originate if not in scripture. As I have stated earlier, it is a Protestant idea, not a scriptural truth. W.A. Jarrel also quotes W.M.F. Warren, D.D., President of Boston University, Methodist:

"The Christian Church is the kingdom of God, viewed in its objective or institutional form." "In

---

1 Jarrel, W.A., *Baptist Church Perpetuity*, The Baptist History Series, pg. 4-5, The Baptist Standard Bearer.

an earlier period, this kingdom was identified as the church . . . The Protestants regarded it . . . as the Christian institution of salvation."[1] i.e. *Universal* Church.

I.K. Cross in The Battle for Baptist History states,

"Obviously the idea of a mystical body referring to the 'whole church,' commonly accepted by Protestant thinking, is an improvision created during the Reformation to accommodate Rome's daughters."[2]

To begin with, the title "Catholic" means of course *Universal*. The idea of the Catholic Church however was a *Universal Visible Church* outside of which there was no salvation. When the reformer Martin Luther came along and protested the Church of Rome, it wasn't long until he found himself outside the apostate church. Therefor Luther, building on Augustine's concepts moved away from the teaching of a *Universal Catholic Visible Church* to the idea of a

---

[1] Jarrel, W.A., *Baptist Church Perpetuity*, The Baptist History Series, pg. 6, The Baptist Standard Bearer.

[2] Cross, I.K., *The Battle for Baptist History*, Bogard Press, pg. 12.

Universal Invisible Church[1] said to consist of the redeemed of all ages. Convenient, since he now found himself outside of the "church" of which it was said there is no salvation outside of. So, what then made a person a member of this *Invisible Universal Church*, which, up to this point seemed to be defined by everyone as a local body of believers? Luther then forced the interpretation of *Spirit Baptism* into the *Universal Church* upon 1st Corinthians 12:13. Thus *Holy Spirit Baptism into the Universal Church* is a protestant fallacy as admitted by the above Methodist. The modern Baptist acceptance of the protestant view of 1st Corinthians 12:13, is not biblical, nor is it the historical Baptist view. John T. Christian states;

"The Roman Catholics have always denied the existence of a universal spiritual church. Until the German Reformation [Luther] there was practically no other conception of a church. [But that of a local congregation of baptized believers] When Luther and others split off from the Roman Catholic Church, a new interpretation of

---

[1] http://www.bbcn.org/filerequest/2135

this passage [Matthew 16:18] was adopted to suit the new views..."[1]

"The errant doctrine of baptismal salvation was indeed one of the first to enter into Christendom. It was later incorporated into the platform of Catholicism. The Protestant reformers of the Catholic system carried on this belief in the form of a 'spiritual sacrament.' This is altogether different from the sealing of the Holy Spirit, which we receive at salvation (Eph. 1:13; 4:30). It is a mystical progression from one unbiblical notion (baptism as a means of grace) to another. If salvation now involves a mystical, invisible baptism into a mystical, invisible 'church' then you have the same spirit of error. You also retain the basic premise that 'salvation' is synonymous with a 'church' and therefore mutually interdependent. Biblical baptism, however, is a completely different matter. It is performed as an ordinance of the Lord's New Testament church upon those who have demonstrated the fruits of repentance and profession of faith. The Lord's water baptism is not a picture of another (so-called) 'true-baptism.' That is, it does not represent anything related to the heretical doctrine of baptismal salvation. Therefore, the

---

[1] Christian, John T., *A History of the Baptists*, Volume One., pg. 20, Bogard Press

51

water baptism of those who baptize under that doctrine is another baptism altogether."[1]

Start with the word "church." What does the word in the original language mean, what was the classical or common use of the word and what is the contextual use of the word?

Church – The word "church" is used over 100 times in the New Testament, and with the exception of one instance, (Acts 19:37) the same Greek word was chosen by the Holy Spirit, which word is *ekklesia*. Strongs 1577, "a calling out, a congregation, a meeting, an assembly, a church." To further show that *ekklesia* is an assembly, notice the following passages where *ekklesia* is translated as "assembly," (Acts 19:32; Acts 19:39; Acts 19:41). When Jesus said, "I will build my church," this is the same word chosen by the Holy Spirit. Why take a word chosen by the infallible God and ascribe a meaning to it that it does not convey?

Hebrews 2:12 also aids in rightly interpreting the word church, "in the midst of the church will I sing praise unto thee." This is a restatement of the Messianic prophecy found in

---

[1] Porter, Les., *Baptist Baptism: A Heritage of Scriptural Authority Vs. The Corruption of Popular Practice.*, pg. 36 (Les Porter & Mac Woody).

Psalm 22:22 where the word congregation is used, so that a church is a congregation!

Words mean something. "Holy men of God spake as they were moved by the Holy Ghost." We speak using words. Books contain paragraphs, thoughts and sentences, none of which are possible without words. The Holy Spirit of God selected the words, and "every Word of God is pure."

The classical or common use *ekklesia* – The meaning of words does change over time, so it is important to discover what exactly was the meaning of the word as it was used when the Bible was written. The Bible gives us the answer for this as the word *ekklesia* being used over 100 times translated church or churches, but on three occasions *ekklesia* was translated assembly. Is it not evident that the word *ekklesia* as it was used then meant assembly? The word *ekklesia*, meaning "called out assembly" did not in its common usage indicate the purpose for the assembly. However, the New Testament makes it clear the purposes of Christian assembly. Concerning the other three accounts where *ekklesia* is translated assembly, context shows the reason for the assembly, but it is always assembly. "Ecclesia, Greek Ekklēsia, ("gathering of those summoned"), in ancient

Greece, assembly of citizens in a city-state. Its roots lay in the Homeric agora, the meeting of the people."[1] James Pendleton stated:

"The Greek term *ekklesia* – translated "church" more than a hundred times in the New Testament (rendered "assembly" three times) – is compounded of two words literally meaning 'to call out of.' ... My present purpose is answered by the statement that in apostolic times a church was composed of persons who had been called out from the world, even as Christ chose his Apostles 'out of the world.' They had been called from the bondage of sin into the liberty of the gospel; from spiritual darkness into the light of salvation; from the dominion of unbelief into the realm of faith; from an heirship of wrath to an heirship of glory. This was true of the members of the first churches. Brought by the Holy Spirit into a new relation to God through Christ, they were prepared for church-relations and church-membership. This preparation was moral, consisting of 'repentance toward God and faith toward our Lord Jesus Christ.' But repentance and faith are exercises of the mind and are consequently invisible. They are private between God and the soul. The world knows not

---

[1] https://www.britannica.com/topic/Ecclesia-ancient-Greek-assembly

of them. Churches, however, are visible organizations. This being the case, there must be some visible ceremonial qualification for membership. This qualification is baptism. There can, according to the Scriptures, be no visible church without baptism .... That baptized believers are the only persons eligible for church-membership is clear from the whole tenor of the Acts of the Apostles and of the Apostolic Epistles. Everywhere it is seen that baptism preceded church-relations; nor is there an intimation that it was possible for an unbaptized person to be a church-member."[1]

"In 1544 the Waldenses [Baptist Ancestors], in order to remove the prejudice which was entertained against them ... transmitted to the king of France, in writing, a Confession of Faith. Article seven says of baptism: 'We believe that in the ordinance of baptism the water is the visible and external sign, which represents to us that which, by virtue of God's invisible operation, is within us, the renovation of our minds, and the mortification of our members through (the faith of) Jesus Christ. And by this ordinance we are

---

[1] Pendleton, James. M., *Distinctive Principles of Baptists*, pg. 170-171,
Philadelphia: American Baptist Publication Society, The Baptist Standard Bearer, Inc.

received into the holy congregation of God's people, previously professing our faith and the change of life."[1] Were these not Baptists, and do we not who are Baptist proclaim the same truth today?

Consider the contextual use of the word *ekklesia* "church." – It is a clear fact that in every passage in which the Universalist finds his "church" *Universal* he must do damage to the context to make it such. For in every instance where the Church is referred to as being *Universal*, the context is that of a *local* church, or the totality of churches in the aggregate.

➢ Matthew 16:18, "I will build my church; and the gates of hell shall not prevail against it." It is suggested that the church Jesus is speaking of here is a *Universal* Church. But how, without presupposing the Church is *Universal* instead of a *local visible* body of believers does one come to this conclusion? Who was Jesus speaking to? He was speaking to what was His Church at that time, the Apostles, who were the first gifts to

1 Christian, John T., *A History of the Baptists*, Volume One., pg. 78, Bogard Press.

the Church, and since they were called, assembled, and ordained prior to Pentecost, they therefore of necessity constituted the Church at this time. Jesus was indeed speaking to His Church and no doubt had in mind the same idea that is conveyed through the word chosen by the Holy Spirit of God, *ekklesia*. To further prove this point, the next instance where Jesus speaks concerning His Church involves disciplinary action. In Matthew 18:17, "And if he shall neglect to hear them, tell *it* unto the church: but if he neglect to hear the church, let him be unto thee as an heathen man and a publican." Jesus is clearly and plainly here speaking of the Church *local*.

"The first church was organized by Jesus and his apostles; and after the form of this one all other churches should be modeled. The churches so organized are to continue in the world until the kingdoms of this earth shall become the kingdom of our Lord, even Christ. Prophecy was full of the enduring character of the kingdoms of Christ (Daniel 2:44,45), Jesus maintained a like view of his church and extended the promise to all ages, He said: 'Upon this rock I will build my church; and the gates of hell shall not prevail against it' (Matthew 16:18). The word church here is doubtless used in its ordinary, literal sense as a local institution; and in the other passage where it is found in Matthew 18:17 it must be taken with the same signification. The great mass of scholarship supports the contention that this passage refers to the local, visible church of Christ."[1]

➢ 1st Corinthians 12:13, "For by one Spirit are we all baptized into one body." This is the much disputed Vs. that is supposed to teach Baptism by the Spirit into the *Universal Church*. However, one must ignore that fact that the Apostle Paul is writing to a *local* church concerning the members relationship to each other within that *local* body of believers. Paul uses the metaphor of a body, and what could be more *local* and *visible* than a body. Therefore, plain and simple interpretation sees that "body" spoken of by Paul to be the *local* body of believers at Corinth. Does he swap back and forth between speaking of the nature of the relationship between believers in a *local* body to speaking about some *invisible* body of believers that could never suffer and rejoice together? Baptism *with* the Holy Spirit *by*

1 Christian, John T., *A History of the Baptists*, Volume One., pg. 20, Bogard Press.

Jesus will be discussed later. But for now, notice that this baptism can only be the "one baptism" spoken of in Ephesians 4:5, which baptism can only be the baptism the Lord's Church was commissioned to administer to believers in the Great Commission in Matthew 28:18-20. Otherwise there would be "two" baptisms. The interpretation then is this, the same Spirit that leads one to salvation will lead the same to follow Christ in water baptism, thereby uniting him with some local body of believers. Examples: "And he came by the Spirit into the Temple," Luke 2:27, & "AND Jesus being full of the Holy Ghost returned from Jordan, and was led by the Spirit into the wilderness" Luke 4:1. The Spirit did not place Simeon in the Temple or Jesus in the Wilderness, the Spirit led them there. "The Holy Spirit testifies, in the same connection, that they were saved before they were baptized [Acts 2:41] "And the Lord added to the church daily those who were saved" ---- or "the saved." Baptism is the only Lord's-appointed way of adding to His Church; for says Paul: "In [by] one Spirit (i.e., of joyful obedience and submissive faith) were we (the Apostles and all whom he addressed, as well as every Christian that should in time after read the epistle) all baptized into one body (a local church), and were all made to drink of one Spirit." This cannot refer to "baptism in the Holy Ghost and in fire," since neither Paul nor the Corinthian Christians had ever been baptized in the Holy Ghost, nor have we in this age."[1]

➢ Ephesians 5:23-25, "For the husband is the head of the wife, even as Christ is the head of the church: and he is the Saviour of the body. Therefore as the church is subject unto Christ, so *let* the wives be to their own husbands in every thing. Husbands, love your wives, even as Christ also loved the church, and gave himself for it." Now the *Universal Church Proponents* assert that the church mentioned here is the church *Universal,* the body, the Bride of Christ. However, we must again remember who Paul is speaking to, and what Paul is speaking about. He is speaking to a *local* church and is speaking concerning an institution, or all churches in general but no church in particular. For instance, which husband and wife was Paul referring to? Some *universal* husband or wife? Or was he speaking concerning the institution of marriage? Obviously, he was speaking concerning the

---

[1] Graves, J.R., *John's Baptism*, Bogard Press, pg. 104-105.

60

institution of marriage and the relationship between each husband and wife, and in comparison, the local church and its relationship to Christ. Was he speaking concerning one specific husband and wife, or all in general? Obviously, he was speaking to all in general. In this same sense he is speaking concerning the Church. Not some *Universal Church,* but all churches in general, or the Church as an institution, which institution cannot exist without the many local churches composing it.

BAPTISM *WITH* OR *BY* THE SPIRIT?

Now to take it one step farther. If the church is *Universal,* what is it that places a person in the *Universal body,* which two words bear no semblance in meaning? The *Universal Church Proponent* then proceeds to take passages referring to water baptism and force the presupposition of *Baptism by the Spirit* upon them. How foolish one's conjecture becomes when they impose their presuppositions upon scripture rather than letting the scriptures speak for themselves. Now notice that there are only 6 references in all of scripture that mentions Baptism *with* the Spirit *by* Jesus. But notice well that in each of these it is not the Spirit baptizing, but rather Jesus baptizing *with* the Spirit!

1. Matthew 3:11, "I indeed baptize you with water unto repentance: but he that cometh after me is mightier than I, whose shoes I am not worthy to bear: he shall baptize you with the Holy Ghost and *with* fire:"

2. Mark 1:8, "I indeed have baptized you with water: but he shall baptize you with the Holy Ghost."

3. Luke 3:16, "John answered, saying unto *them* all, I indeed baptize you with water; but

one mightier than I, that latchet of whose shoes I am not worthy to unloose: he shall baptize you with the Holy Ghost and with fire:"

4. John 1:33, "And I knew him not: but he that sent me to baptize with water, the same said unto me, Upon whom thou shalt see the Spirit descending, and remaining on him, the same is he which baptizeth with the Holy Ghost."

5. Acts 1:5, "For John truly baptized with water; but ye shall be baptized with the Holy Ghost not many days hence."

6. Acts 11:16, "Then remembered I the word of the Lord, how that he said, John indeed baptized with water; but ye shall be baptized with the Holy Ghost."

Now it should be clear that in these six references, which is all there is, that Jesus was the one who would baptize *with* the Spirit. But when, where and to whom was this promise made? Luke 24:49, "And, behold, I send the promise of my Father upon you: but tarry ye in the city of Jerusalem, until ye be endued with power from on high." Luke records the promise of Christ, which promise was made to His Church, and the purpose for which was in order that His Church would be endued with Power from on high. Looking to Acts, the writer Luke picks up where he leaves off in his gospel account we find these words. "And, being assembled together with *them*, commanded them that they should not depart from Jerusalem, but wait for the promise of the Father, which, *saith he*, ye have heard of me. For John truly baptized with water; but ye shall be baptized with the Holy Ghost not many days hence. . . . But ye shall receive power, after that the Holy Ghost is come upon you: and ye shall be witnesses unto me both in Jerusalem, and in all Judaea, and in Samaria, and unto the uttermost part of the earth" (Acts 1:4-5 & 8). Now the promise of the Father could not have been fulfilled when Jesus breathed on his disciples and said, "Receive ye the Holy Ghost," as Acts 1:5 states that this was yet unfilled as it would happen "not many days hence." But notice also the clear and stated purpose of the Baptism *by* Jesus *with* the Holy Ghost; it was to give Power to the Lord's Church to carry out the Gospel Commission. Notice the statement in Luke 24:49, "until ye be endued with power," and also Acts 1:8, "But ye shall receive power." The clear and intended purpose was to give *power* to the already existent Church, but never to give *placement* in the Church. In every reference it is clear that Jesus would be the one baptizing and that the Church was the one being baptized, and that they were being baptized *with* the Spirit rather than being baptized *by* the Spirit. The purpose for which was to give power to go into all the world and preach the gospel which is also clear from Acts 1:8. So it is then clear, the forced and incorrectly imposed interpretation of *believers being baptized by the Spirit into the universal body of Christ* was a result of a misunderstanding of the nature of the Lord's True Church. The *Universal Church Proponent* then applies, incorrectly, *Baptism by the Spirit*, which is nowhere in scripture, to passages that speak to the "one" baptism Christ commissioned His Church to continue. Following are a few quotes concerning passages referring to water baptism where the Universalist will impose his *Baptism by the Spirit* upon.

"In the ordinance of baptism there is a profession of faith in Jesus Christ, as we may learn from Eph. 4:5: 'One Lord, one faith, one baptism.' The term 'Lord' in this passage, as is generally the case of the Epistles, refers to Christ. He, having died and risen again, is presented in the gospel as the Object of faith and the Author of salvation. Faith is a trustful acceptance of Christ as the Saviour. On a profession of this 'one faith' in the 'one Lord,' the 'one baptism' is administered. Baptism is therefore a profession of faith." .... Of baptism it may be said that it represents the burial and resurrection of Jesus Christ. This we learn from the following passages: 'Know ye not that so many of us as were baptized into Jesus Christ were baptized into his death? Therefore we are buried with him by baptism into death; that like as Christ was raised up from the dead by the glory of the Father, even so we also should walk in newness of life. For if we have been planted together in the likeness of his death, we shall be also in the likeness of his resurrection;' 'Buried with him in baptism, wherein also ye are raised with him, through the faith of the operation of God, who hath raised him from the dead;' ....It is clear from these passages that baptism has a commemorative reference to the burial and resurrection of Christ."[1] James M. Pendleton

The modern Baptist acceptance of the protestant view of 1st Corinthians 12:13, is not biblical, nor is it the historical Baptist view. In 1802, Pastor T.B. Montanye, representing the

[1] Pendleton, James. M., *Distinctive Principles of Baptists*, pg. 113, Philadelphia: American Baptist Publication Society, The Baptist Standard Bearer, Inc.

elders of the Philadelphia Association, wrote a work on "The Baptism of the Holy Ghost." This work was signed by order of the Association.

"The Baptism of the Holy Ghost ... was never inculcated ...[as] the work of regeneration and sanctification...in the gospel, and we think ought not to be considered as constituting any part in the office work of the Divine Spirit in renewing the heart... [O]ur respected [non-Baptist but Christian] friends...may be regenerated, and enjoy the highest consolation in the sweet incomes of the Holy Comforter, and the most sensible union with Christ; yet as all this does not constitute the baptism of the Holy Spirit, not is designed by it in the sacred scriptures, it follows in consequence, that, rejecting the water baptism, they have no baptism whatever, and ought cheerfully to submit to that prescribed in the example of Jesus Christ...[T]here is no well found evidence of [the] present existence...of the baptism of the Holy Ghost....The term baptism of the Holy Ghost...was first taught by the harbinger of Jesus Christ, Matthew 3:11, "He shall baptize you with the Holy Ghost and with fire" ... the accomplishment of the promise made by Jesus Christ [of the Spirit Baptism was in]...Acts 2:16-22 ...[as prescribed in Luke 24:49]...Acts

68

1:4,5........... Here it is proper to remove some apparent difficulties, which are a means of puzzling the minds of many. First, What baptism the apostle denominates one baptism? We answer, The instituted appointment of Jesus Christ, which he authorized after his resurrection, which remains a standing ordinance in the church, and which Peter, when filled with the Holy Ghost, enjoined on Cornelius and the rest of the believing Gentiles..............In 1st Corinthians....there seems no absurdity in saying that the same Spirit influences all nations to yield an obedience to the instituted appointments of Jesus Christ, and so come [by immersion in water] into the union of the body of Christ..............As for sundry other Scriptures, such as Romans 6:3-4; Colossians 2:12; 1st Peter 3:21; Galatians 3:27; they have an evident relation to water baptism, and are no way connected with, nor yet refer to, the work of grace in the heart."[1]

Consider yet another statement provided to us by Texas Baptists in the 19th century.

---

[1] Quoted from , Thomas D., *Spirit Baptism: A Completed Historical Event*, pg. 61-62. From the minutes of the October 5-7 meeting of Philadelphia Baptist Association, is found on pages 415-420. Baptist Standard Bearer, 2005.

"When the Holy Spirit came with power upon the disciples on the day of Pentecost (Acts 2:2), and fell on the house of Cornelius (Acts 11:15-16), while Peter preached to them, it was called a baptism of the Holy Ghost. In both cases, and all cases of such baptism, speaking with tongues followed...The ordinary operation of the Holy Spirit in the first century, in the regeneration and conversion of men was [not] called a baptism ... of the Spirit.... To speak of the operation of the Holy Spirit in regeneration and conversion as the baptism of the Holy Spirit, is both unscriptural and misleading. For it is not a baptism, even figuratively."[1]

And again, Thomas D. Ross states in his work *Spirit Baptism, A Completed Historical Event*,

"Considering specifically 1st Corinthians 12:13, one notes that the Baptist Confession of 1527 affirmed the faith of all Baptists accepting the document that being "baptized into one body" referred to that immersion in water by which

---

[1] Quoted from Ross, Thomas D., Spirit Baptism: A Completed Historical Event, pg. 62-63. From Texas Historical and Biographical Magazine, vol. 1, ed. John B. Link (1825-1894), elec. Acc. Baptist History Collection....Baptist Standard Bearer, 2005.

one joined the membership of the local, visible assembly"[1]

"The Georgia Baptist Association of Elders and Brethren, to the Churches which they represent, send Christian salutation [In 1828]... We now advance some plain bible proof of that gospel order observed by us.... We believe that water baptism and the Lord's Supper, are ordinances of the Lord, and are to be continued till his second coming. That true believers in Jesus Christ are the only subjects of baptism, and that dipping is the mode. That none but regularly baptized church members have a right to commune at the Lord's Table. In vindication of these doctrines we bring the following plain scriptures: ....For by one Spirit are we all baptized into one body, whether we be Jews or Gentiles, whether we be bond or free..."[2]

Simon Menno (Menno Simons), according to John T. Christian, although ordained a Catholic priest became a convert of the Baptist

[1] Ross, Thomas D., *Spirit Baptist: A Completed Historical Event.*, pg. 63

[2] Ross, Thomas D., *Spirit Baptist: A Completed Historical Event.*, pg. 63., Pg. 175-181, *History of the Georgia Baptist Association*, Jesse Mercer. Washington, GA, pub. 1838. Elec. Acc. *Baptist History Collection.*

faith in 1531. Menno became a great Baptist leader during his time. In his writings, the passage in Romans 6:1-3, is found over 100 times. In the following, Menno uses Romans 6 in obvious reference to water baptism.

"Observe all of you who persecute the word of the Lord and his people, this is our instruction, doctrine and belief concerning baptism, according to the instruction of the words of Christ, namely, we must first hear the word of God, believe, and then upon our faith be baptized; ..... To God be eternal praise; we will know that the word of the Lord teaches us and testifies to, on the subject. The word of the Lord commands us that we, with sincere hearts, desire to die to sin, to bury our sins with Christ, and with him to arise to a new life, even as baptism is portrayed."[1]

Menno quotes 1st Corinthians 12:13 as sustaining the practice of immersion. He says,

"Moses believed the word of the Lord, and erected a serpent; Israel looked upon it and was healed, not through the virtue of the image, but through the power of the divine word, received

---

[1] Christian, John T., *A History of the Baptists*, Volume One. Pg. 143-144. Bogard Press

72

by them through faith. In the same manner salvation is ascribed in scriptural baptism Mark 16:16 the forgiveness of sins, Acts 2:38, the putting on of Christ, Gal. 3:27, being dipped into one body, 1st Corinthians 12:13."[1] *(Notice that Romans 6:3-4, 1st Cor. 12:13, Gal. 3:27, were all understood to be references to water baptism.)*

In a Baptist confession of faith dated to 1536 an obvious reference to Romans 6 is made concerning water baptism, as well as it being the doorway to the church.

"The dipping, as the Apostles write it, and also used the same, is to be performed with this understanding. They also who are dipped are therein to confess their faith, and, by virtue of this faith, to be disposed to put off the old man, and henceforth to live in a new conversation; indeed, it is on this condition that the dipping is to be received, by every candidate that he, with the certain announcement of a good conscience, renewed and born again through the Holy Ghost, will forsake all unrighteousness with all works of darkness, and will die to them. And, accordingly, the dipping is a burial of the old man and a raising up of the new man; likewise a door into the holy church, and a putting on of

---

[1] Christian, John T., *A History of the Baptists*, Volume One. Pg. 143-144. Bogard Press

Jesus Christ. ... that the dipping is an immersion in water, which the candidate desires and receives as a token that he has died to sin, has been buried with Christ, thereby risen to a new life, thenceforth to walk not in the lust of the flesh, but obediently according to the will of God. They who are thus minded and thus confess, the same should be dipped."[1] *(Romans 6:3-4, "Know ye not, that so many of us as were baptized into Jesus Christ were baptized into his death? Therefore we are buried with him by baptism into death: that like as Christ was raised up from the dead by the glory of the Father, even so we also should walk in newness of life.")*

In the early 1600's Baptist preacher John Norcott wrote a book which was later edited and published by Charles Spurgeon in defense of baptism by immersion. Notice the following expressions relating to water baptism.

"Baptism signifies the burial of Christ. Therefore we are buried with him by baptism into death, Romans 6:4. Buried with him in baptism, Col. 2:12. Now do we reckon a man buried when a little earth is sprinkled on his face, but he is buried when covered; we are buried in

---

[1] Christian, John T., *A History of the Baptists*, Volume One. Pg. 165-166. Bogard Press

baptism... Baptism is the putting on of Christ. As many of you as have been baptized into Christ have put on Christ, Gal. 3:27."[1]

Let's reach further back with one final example. The Baptist Historian David Benedict concluded the Donatists (AD 311) were Baptists. Using Augustine's writing, who was a contemporary of the Donatists, he shows that Augustine makes the Donatists Baptist. These same were called Ana-Baptist later in 1605. John T. Christian gives us this information concerning their view of "One Lord, One Faith, and One Baptism."

"Our modern Anabaptists [1607] are the same as the Donatists of old [311 AD]....These rigid moralists, however, did not count themselves Anabaptist; for they thought that there was one Lord, one faith, one baptism and that their own ... They took no account of the baptism of others, and contended that they were wrongly called Anabaptists."[2]

_____

[1] Christian, John T., *A History of the Baptists,* Volume One., Bogard Press. Pg. 240.

[2] Christian, John T., *A History of the Baptists*, Volume One. Pg. 46. Bogard Press

It's clear that these ancient Baptist believed the "one baptism" was water baptism. It is also clear that they believed that "baptism" belonged to them and no one else. They rejected the name Anabaptist on the account that they did not consider themselves to be re-baptizing anyone, but that they were justly and rightly administering baptism in the first place.

J.R. Graves writes in *John's Baptism*,

"There is but one body in heaven or on earth that we can be baptized into, and that is this local, visible organization of baptized believers in Christ Jesus our Lord .... Understand the 'body of Christ' [1st Corinthians 12:13] here to refer to a local church, and it meets all the requirements of the passage and its connections ---Paul's beautiful comparison of the human body and its members, and the local church and its members; but to understand it of a Church Invisible, it meets none of the requirements of the passage or comparison. The Holy Ghost never baptized any one into either the visible or an invisible church. Water baptism does add to a real visible church, and nothing else does. But an invisible administrator invisibly baptizing invisible subjects into an invisible church, sounds to me like visible nonsense. Can my reader for one moment think that the Holy Spirit ever taught Paul and all the Christians of his age were immersed into a Conception? A huge FIGRUE OF SPEECH?!? Let Pedobaptists teach thus, if they will, to avoid the teachings of the Holy Spirit; but Baptists --- never."[1]

---

[1] Graves, J.R., *John's Baptism*, Bogard Press, pg. 81-82

DANGERS OF THE UNIVERSAL CHURCH DOCTRINE (THEORY)

1. As it is not found in scripture, but imposed upon it, it becomes destructive in its very nature to the true teaching concerning the Lord's Church. It is, in its very essence, the exact opposite of the True Church of Christ. *Universal* and *Assembly* stand in opposition to each other. It may be one or the other, but it cannot be both!

2. It is destructive to the correct observance of the ordinances Christ gave to His Church. The ordinances are local church ordinances, established by Christ and delivered to His church(es). Paul writing to the local church at Corinth says, "Keep the ordinances as I have delivered them unto you." If a person believes the church is *Universal,* they should practice *open* communion; they would be wrong, but at least consistent in their beliefs! The Bible teaches Communion as a local church ordinance and not to be observed outside the discipline of each local church.

3. It is destructive to Local Church Authority, Matt. 28:18-20. Some Pastors accepting this view believe they have authority to baptize outside of the authority of a local church. And why wouldn't they, if the church is

Universal rather than *Local* and we are all one body, wherever a saved person is the body is, and has as much right as anyone else to do anything at all. They are wrong, but at least they are consistently wrong.

4. It is destructive to proper biblical mission work. Missionaries are called by God, endorsed and supported by the Local church (Acts 13:1-3 & Acts 14:26-27). Missionaries, to do the mission work of God, require the endorsement of a local church. However, it is a regular occurrence today, even among "Baptists," to without any endorsing local church, to start "their" own new church. And why wouldn't they have a right to do just that, if the church is *Universal*, and the authority Christ gave His church[es) was instead given to a church *Universal?*

5. It is destructive to the exhortation to "forsake not the assembling of ourselves together." "Why go to church, we are the church" is the mindset of many today. Where did that come from? The candid observer can see the damage this false doctrine has caused. Christians today believe that every believer has all the authority to accomplish and do all that Christ commissioned His Church to do. Such as, start a church, or wherever I am the

church is, or baptize someone etc. People think church is Bible study around a campfire, and why wouldn't it be if the church is *Universal*? I hear my Baptist friends who would like to have it both ways, *Universal* and *Local* say to me, "The reason campfire Bible study isn't church is because that isn't what Christ established!!" You are correct, it isn't what Christ established. Tell me then what did He establish, two things unalike and call them both the "church?"

6. It is counterproductive to everything the Lord commissioned His Church to do. Tell me, can the *Church Universal* collect an offering for a missionary, call a Pastor, select Deacons, hold a service, Baptize anyone, practice discipline, etc? Of course not! But you say that's the work of the church "local." It is, but would God set up two kinds of "churches?" Would God in His wisdom establish one kind of church to do His work and another unseen that logically weakens the work of the Local church?

7. It is counterproductive to the efforts to keep the Lord's Church pure and separate from the institutions of men. It lends itself to ecumenicalism. If the Lord's Church (Baptist) has no historical ties to the New Testament

Christianity any more than any other "church," if we are the product of the Protestant Reformation and if the True Church is *Universal,* on what grounds do we have to separate ecclesiastically with any other "church?"

SOME THOUGHTS IN CONCLUSION

1. A visible church of Christ is a congregation of scripturally baptized believers, associated together by covenant in the faith and fellowship of the gospel; observing the ordinances of Christ; governed by His laws; and exercising the gifts, rights and privileges invested in them by His Word.

2. There can, according to scriptures, be no visible church without baptism. Or, as J. R. Graves stated, "By this simple test human societies, and all counterfeit churches, can be easily distinguished from the churches of Christ, vis., in the former, water is put before the blood, and the church before Christ; in the latter Christ is put before the church, and the blood before the water."[1] Blood before the

---

[1] Graves, J.R., *Old Landmarkism: What is it?*, pg. 53, Solid Christian Books.

water, water before the church. When is baptism scriptural? 1) Proper Candidate, believers only, 2) Proper mode, immersion, 3) Proper authority, the churches organized after the model left by Christ, and only scriptural Baptist churches retain this authority.

3. When the church is used in a general or institutional sense it speaks of the Lord's churches in the aggregate, but never of a *universal* body of believers.

4. The Lord organized His Church during His personal ministry, authorized that Church to carry out the Great commission of evangelizing the world, baptizing believers, and to teach them the "all things" of Christ.

5. The Lord promised the perpetual existence of His churches, "the gates of hell shall not prevail against it."

6. Each church is an autonomous body with Christ as its head and has a right to do whatever the scripture gives it a right to do.

7. The Ordinances were given to the local church and as such should never be extended outside the discipline of each body. The rights and privileges of each church belong only to the members of that body.

8. The scripture also speaks of the family of God, the whole family of heaven and earth, which includes the redeemed of all ages. Galatians 3:26, "For ye are all the children of God by faith in Christ Jesus." But not all of these belong to the church, but, "For as many of you as have been baptized into Christ have put on Christ" Gal. 3:27.

9. While all who are saved belong to "whole family of heaven and earth," all who are saved have not been baptized. But, "as many as have been" baptized have united with a local church, and therefore belong to His church, His body, His bride. "And, other sheep I have, which are not of this fold" John 10:16.

Sadly, there are Pastors today standing behind the pulpits in what were historically "Landmark Missionary Baptist Churches," preaching, if indeed they are bold enough to do so, an ecclesiastical doctrine that is not only foreign to scripture, but foreign to the Articles of Faith accepted by the church they serve. They are indeed, knowingly or not, laboring to subvert the very nature and with that the very structure and scriptural observances and practices of the Lord's Church. Many of them know they labor in churches, and many of those churches in associations that have clear and stated ecclesiastical beliefs that are not in harmony with their own. They may be good men, they may be sincere men, but they are ecclesiastical wolves in sheep's clothing. If they, being those who accept the notion of a church *Universal,* are willing to be consistent, then they should throw of the garment of Missionary Baptist Identity, open communion up to all, lay aside any ecclesiastical boundaries they have and be in practice what they are in doctrine.

"Many Baptists have traded the apostolic faith for the deluding influence of ecumenical, Protestant fundamentalism. Since baptism is not a "fundamental of the faith" it is effectively marginalized – and therefore Protestantized."[1] "Baptists have been betrayed into the hands of Protestantism by their own historians. While Protestantism failed in the sixteenth and seventeenth centuries to destroy them by fire and imprisonment, they have succeeded in the twentieth century through compromise and the rewriting of history in corrupting much of Baptist life."[2]

---

1 Les Porter, *Baptist Baptism: A Heritage of Scriptural Authority Vs. The Corruption of Popular Practice.,* pg.32. (Les Porter & Mac Woody)

2 Cross, I.K., *The Battle for Baptist History,* Bogard Press, pg. 7.

What came out of Rome

will eventually lead back to Rome!

THE ORIGIN OF COUNTERFEIT CHURCHES

(This List is not comprehensive)

Roman Catholic progressively developed by Constantine, Sylvester I, Loe I, Gregory I.

Eastern Orthodox split from Rome in 869 AD – Patriarch Photius.

Lutheran split from Rome in 1517 AD – Martin Luther, Germany.

Mennonite split from Anabaptist in 1525 AD – Menno Simons, Switzerland.

Church of England split from Rome in 1534 AD – Henry VII, England.

Reformed split from Rome in 1534 AD - John Calvin, Switzerland.

Presbyterian split from Rome in 1560 AD – John Knox, Scotland.

Congregational split from Church of England – Robert Browne in   1560 AD.

Quakers split from Church of England – George Fox, England.

Moravian Brethren split from Lutheran in 1727 AD - Nicolas Von Zinzendorf, Germany.

Methodist split from Church of England in 1740 AD –

Charles Wesley, England.

Church of Christ / Disciples of Christ split from Baptists in 1860 AD – Alexander Campbell, USA.

Plymouth Brethren split from Church of England – John Darby.

Salvation Army split from Methodist 1865 AD. Started by William Booth in England

Pentecostalism split from Methodist in 1901 by Charles Parham, USA. William Seymour was a student of Charles Parham and from the Azusa Street Revival in California many Pentecostal groups were later formed.

Four Square was developed from various Pentecostal groups by Aimee McPherson in the USA in 1914.

Assemblies of God was formed in 1914 out of the Azusa Street Revival, which was led by

William Seymour who was a student of Charles Parham.

Oneness Pentecostalism was formed in 1914 – Ewert and Glenn Cook.

United Pentecostal Churches were formed in 1945 by Oneness groups merging together.

Full Gospel churches were formed in 1992 – Bishop Paul S. Morton Sr.
Church of God was formed on August 19th, 1886 by an apostate Baptist minister.

Nazarene split from various Holiness & Methodist groups 1919 in USA.

Bible Churches split from Presbyterian & Congregational. Was started by William McCarrell, USA in 1930.

Mormon church was started on April 6th, 1830 – Joseph Smith.

Jehovah's Witness was started in 1870 – Charles Taze Russell.

BAPTIST – SEASHORES OF GALILEE – JESUS CHRIST

Note: These dates are approximate, because several denominations "emerged" over a period of time. The human founder listed was often associated with other prominent men in the denomination's formation.

Made in the USA
Monee, IL
13 January 2022

88823818R00050